The Blackbird Brothers

I can do it!

Written by

Sonia Richards

Illustrated by

Joanne Bradley

To Raina and Hunter -
You can Do it! a
Sonia R.

This book belongs to

_____

About the Author

Sonia Richards is a Psychoanalytic Psychotherapist and Counsellor.

In her practice in Suffolk she has found that many of the problems brought into her consulting room are similar to the issues talked about in this story and the new *"Message in a Bottle Series"*, a collection of 6 short stories so called because each story is a message and suggests a way of helping children think about differing issues that they may face as they grow up. The stories are written for 3 – 7 year olds, and the books set out in simple language how children might think about their issues in a creative way and to help them recognise that they are not alone with their problems. Sonia believes that the books will sit somewhere in the children's unconscious, and therefore may be useful to call upon at some point.

Sonia wanted to find a way of helping children and their parents think about the problems together and therefore, as picture books, they can be read to younger children whilst allowing older children to read the stories themselves.

THE BLACKBIRD BROTHERS

Timmy and Tommy were baby blackbird brothers, and although they were hatched at more or less the same time they were very different. They lived in a nest perched on top of a yew hedge and the wood pigeons cooed nearby. It felt very safe and peaceful.

But then came the time to leave the nest.

However Timmy was timid.

And Tommy was bold.

And even though Timmy was the first to flutter down rather uncertainly from his nest, all he could do was to call to his mother with a frightened cheep.

"Cheep cheep cheep", he called.

Tommy on the other hand was itching to get down, and was very excited. And when eventually he was allowed to go, he almost swooped down.

"Yippee!!" he shouted.

He landed just behind Timmy but immediately he found his feet and started to run. He flapped his wings gently and almost flew up into the air.

Timmy looked on jealously. No matter how hard he flapped his wings, he did not even lift a millimetre into the air.

His mother encouraged both Timmy and Tommy, "It is really fun" she said, and continued, "In order to fly you need to flap your wings like this."

And she showed them. Suddenly she was up in the air and landed in the apple tree above them.

They looked up and saw her sitting there.

"Wow", said Tommy "I want to do that!"

"It looks very high", said Timmy rather nervously.

Tommy tried and flew six centimetres into the air.

"Hurrah, Hurray, Hurray! This is fun!" He cheeped.

Timmy tried and flapped his wings really hard but all he did was to move a little further forward up the garden. Plop, he stumbled almost on to his beak. He tried again, plop, this time he fell over on to his side.

"I can't do it", he said sadly, "I feel too scared".

"Try again, baby blackbirds", encouraged their mother.

Tommy tried again and this time he flew higher.

"I can do it" He whooped, really excitedly.

Timmy tried once more but only went even further forward up the garden. No matter how hard he flapped his wings he could not get lift off.

"I can't fly", he said again, "I really can't. It is too hard. I will just have to get eaten by the cat instead!" He tweeted piteously.

His mother said gently, "Timmy, if you say you can't you won't, but if you say you can, you will."

Timmy nodded, and tried again.

Nothing happened and then he said out loud, "I can fly."

Nothing happened.

His mother said, "Keep saying it".

Then he flapped his wings really hard.

"I can do it, I can fly" he said again out loud.

"Try again", said his mother gently, "but don't try too hard, just wave your wings like this, (and she showed him), and BELIEVE you will fly!"

"I will fly" said Timmy.

"I can fly! I CAN fly! I CAN FLY!!!"

And then something strange happened and he flew! He flew, up, up in the air and landed rather uncertainly next to his mother on the apple tree branch.

"I can fly too", said Tommy, and perched next to his mother and Timmy. All three settled down for the night until father joined them and Timmy and Tommy both showed off their new found flying skills.

Timmy told his father "I learned that if I really believe I can, I find I can do anything."

His father nodded and smiled at his two sons.

"I am proud of you both," he said, "It is hard to be brave when you are scared, and so it is even braver when you make yourselves do something that scares you. I hope you are both very proud of yourselves".

The brothers nodded and went to sleep very quickly that night high up in the branches of the apple tree.

The End

Bullies NEVER win

The big hairy dog hated cats. He even hated the sight of them. They made him sneeze and wheeze and his eyes water. In fact he felt quite scared of them because as a puppy he was scratched across the face by a stray cat who lived in the shed at the bottom of the garden, and so the big hairy dog had kept away from cats ever since.

The big hairy dog lived with his owner Jane, two doors down from Noggin the cat and Scruff the dog. He liked Scruff and sometimes they played together in the park, but if he saw Noggin he began to feel quite unwell.

And now here was Noggin just sitting outside his front door, - again! He could see Noggin through the glass, licking his paws and then cleaning the back of his ears. As if he had all the time in the world. The big hairy dog felt nervous, his tummy hurt and his mouth felt dry.

This is a story about bullies. It shows that bullies are often scared themselves which is why very often they puff themselves up to feel bigger and braver.

In this story it shows one way that bullies can be tackled. The story emphasises asking for help and NEVER allowing the bully to win.

Printed in Great Britain
by Amazon